Copyright © 2023 by Lily J. Thompson (Author)

This book is protected by copyright law and is intended solely for personal use. Reproduction, distribution, or any other form of use requires the written permission of the author. The information presented in this book is for educational and entertainment purposes only, and while every effort has been made to ensure its accuracy and completeness, no guarantees are made. The author is not providing legal, financial, medical, or professional advice, and readers should consult with a licensed professional before implementing any of the techniques discussed in this book. The content in this book has been sourced from various reliable sources, but readers should exercise their own judgment when using this information. The author is not responsible for any losses, direct or indirect, that may occur from the use of this book, including but not limited to errors, omissions, or inaccuracies.

We hope this book has been informative and helpful on your journey to understanding and celebrating older adults. Thank you for your interest and support!

Title: Demystifying Cancer-A Guide to Understanding Types of Cancer

Subtitle: Symptoms, Treatments, and Personal Experiences from Survivors and Families

Series: Overcoming Cancer: A Journey of Hope

By Lily J. Thompson

Table of Contents

"Cancer can take away all of my physical abilities. It cannot touch my mind, it cannot touch my heart, and it cannot touch my soul."
Jim Valvano

"We can't change the cards we are dealt, just how we play the hand."
Randy Pausch (who died of pancreatic cancer)

"Cancer didn't bring me to my knees, it brought me to my feet."
Michael Douglas (who was successfully treated for throat cancer)

"I am not afraid of dying. I have lived a wonderful life. If I die tomorrow, I have no complaints. I really want to go to Pluto."
Sally Ride (who died of pancreatic cancer)

"The greatest glory in living lies not in never falling, but in rising every time we fall."
Nelson Mandela (who survived prostate cancer)

"My cancer scare changed my life. I'm grateful for every new, healthy day I have. It has helped me prioritize my life."
Olivia Newton-John (who has battled breast cancer multiple times)

"I believe that imagination is stronger than knowledge. That myth is more potent than history. That dreams are more powerful than facts. That hope always triumphs over experience. That laughter is the only cure for grief. And I believe that love is stronger than cancer."
Robert Fulghum

Introduction

Explanation of the purpose and importance of understanding different types of cancer

Cancer is a term that most of us have heard before. We all know someone, whether it be a family member, friend, or acquaintance, who has been affected by this disease in some way. Cancer is a complex disease, and it can be difficult to understand. There are so many different types of cancer, each with their own unique characteristics, symptoms, and treatments.

That's where this book comes in. The purpose of this book is to provide a comprehensive guide to understanding the different types of cancer. We believe that knowledge is power, and that by understanding the different types of cancer, we can better protect ourselves and our loved ones.

First and foremost, understanding the different types of cancer can help with early detection. Early detection is key to successful treatment and recovery. By being aware of the symptoms associated with different types of cancer, individuals can seek medical attention sooner rather than later, potentially catching the cancer at an early stage where it is more easily treatable.

Additionally, understanding the different types of cancer can help individuals make informed decisions about their health. For example, knowing about the risk factors associated with different types of cancer can help individuals make lifestyle choices that may reduce their risk of developing cancer.

Moreover, by understanding the different types of cancer, individuals can better support their loved ones who may be going through a cancer diagnosis or treatment. Knowing what to expect can help individuals provide emotional support and practical assistance to those in need.

Finally, this book aims to provide hope. Despite the seriousness of cancer, there are new and emerging treatments being developed every day. By staying up-to-date on the latest research and treatments, individuals can maintain a sense of hope and optimism.

In conclusion, understanding the different types of cancer is crucial for our health, our loved ones, and our future. This book is designed to be an accessible and informative resource for anyone looking to learn more about cancer and its various types.

Overview of the contents of the book and what readers can expect to learn

Now that we've discussed the importance of understanding different types of cancer, let's dive into what you can expect to learn from this book. We have organized the contents of this book into several chapters, each focusing on a specific type of cancer.

Chapter 1 provides an introduction to the concept of cancer and how it develops. We also discuss the different types of cancer, including carcinomas, sarcomas, leukemias, and lymphomas, and their prevalence and incidence.

Chapter 2 focuses on carcinomas, which are the most common type of cancer. We provide an in-depth explanation of the different subtypes of carcinomas, such as basal cell carcinoma, squamous cell carcinoma, and adenocarcinoma, and discuss the causes and risk factors associated with each subtype. We also provide an overview of the symptoms and diagnostic tests used to detect carcinomas, as well as the treatments available for each subtype, including surgery, radiation therapy, chemotherapy, and immunotherapy.

Chapter 3 is all about sarcomas, which are less common than carcinomas but still require understanding. We provide an in-depth explanation of the different subtypes of sarcomas, such as osteosarcoma, chondrosarcoma, and liposarcoma, and discuss the causes and risk factors associated with each subtype. We also provide an overview of the symptoms and diagnostic tests used to detect sarcomas, as well as the treatments available for each subtype, including surgery, radiation therapy, chemotherapy, and immunotherapy.

Chapter 4 focuses on leukemias, which are cancers of the blood cells. We provide an in-depth explanation of the different types of leukemias, such as acute lymphoblastic leukemia, chronic lymphocytic leukemia, and acute myeloid leukemia, and discuss the causes and risk factors associated with each type. We also provide an overview of the symptoms and diagnostic tests used to detect leukemias, as well as the treatments available for each type, including chemotherapy, radiation therapy, bone marrow transplantation, and immunotherapy.

Chapter 5 is all about lymphomas, which are cancers of the lymphatic system. We provide an in-depth explanation of the different types of lymphomas, such as Hodgkin lymphoma and non-Hodgkin lymphoma, and discuss the causes and risk factors associated with each type. We also provide an overview of the symptoms and diagnostic tests used to detect lymphomas, as well as the treatments available for each type, including chemotherapy, radiation therapy, targeted therapy, and immunotherapy.

Finally, in Chapter 6, we discuss the latest research and advances in cancer treatment. We provide an overview of new and emerging therapies, such as CAR T-cell therapy and targeted therapy, and explain the importance of clinical trials in developing new cancer treatments. We also include personal stories and interviews with cancer patients and survivors who have undergone these new treatments.

In conclusion, this book is designed to be a comprehensive guide to understanding different types of cancer. We hope that by reading this book, you will gain a better understanding of the various types of cancer, their symptoms, risk factors, and treatments, and be better equipped to protect yourself and your loved ones from this disease.

Discussion of the emotional impact of a cancer diagnosis and how the book can provide support

Receiving a cancer diagnosis can be an overwhelming and emotionally challenging experience for both the patient and their loved ones. The diagnosis may bring up feelings of fear, anxiety, anger, and sadness, among others. It is important to acknowledge and address these emotions and seek the support needed to cope with them.

In this book, we not only aim to provide information about different types of cancer, their symptoms, and treatment options, but also recognize the emotional impact of a cancer diagnosis. We hope to offer support and guidance to those affected by cancer, both patients and their loved ones, as they navigate this difficult journey.

It is normal to experience a wide range of emotions when facing a cancer diagnosis. Patients may feel scared about the future and the uncertainty of their health. They may also feel angry or frustrated with the situation or the treatments they have to undergo. Family members and loved ones may also feel overwhelmed by the news and the impact it can have on their lives.

This book aims to provide emotional support by offering personal experiences from cancer survivors and their families, as well as tips on how to cope with the emotional challenges that come with a cancer diagnosis. We also provide information on support groups, counseling, and other resources available for those who need extra support.

We want readers to know that they are not alone in their journey, and there are resources available to help them cope with the emotional impact of a cancer diagnosis. We believe that providing emotional support alongside information about cancer can help individuals feel more empowered and better equipped to face the challenges ahead.

In summary, this book not only provides information about cancer types, symptoms, and treatments, but also recognizes and addresses the emotional impact of a cancer diagnosis. We hope to offer support and guidance to those affected by cancer and help them cope with the emotional challenges they may face.

Call to action for cancer prevention and early detection

Cancer is a devastating disease that affects millions of people each year. It's a disease that can strike anyone, regardless of age, gender, or lifestyle. However, there are steps we can take to reduce our risk of developing cancer and to detect it early when it does occur.

In this section, we will discuss the importance of cancer prevention and early detection. We will explore the various ways in which you can reduce your risk of developing cancer, as well as the benefits of early detection.

Prevention is key when it comes to cancer. While there are some factors that we cannot control, such as genetics and age, there are many lifestyle changes that we can make to reduce our risk of developing cancer. These include:

- Eating a healthy diet rich in fruits, vegetables, and whole grains

- Maintaining a healthy weight

- Exercising regularly

- Avoiding tobacco and excessive alcohol consumption

- Protecting your skin from the sun

- Getting vaccinated against viruses that can cause cancer, such as HPV and hepatitis B

Early detection is also critical in the fight against cancer. When cancer is detected early, it is often easier to treat and has a better chance of being cured. This is why it's important to be aware of the signs and symptoms of cancer, and to get screened regularly if you are at high risk.

Some common signs and symptoms of cancer include:

- Unexplained weight loss

- Fatigue

- Pain or discomfort that doesn't go away

- Changes in the skin, such as a new mole or a sore that doesn't heal

- Changes in bowel or bladder habits

- Difficulty swallowing

- Persistent cough or hoarseness

If you experience any of these symptoms, it's important to talk to your healthcare provider right away.

Screening tests are also an important tool for early detection. Depending on your age, gender, and other risk factors, your healthcare provider may recommend one or more of the following screening tests:

- Mammography for breast cancer

- Pap test and HPV testing for cervical cancer

- Colonoscopy for colon cancer

- PSA testing for prostate cancer

- Skin exams for skin cancer

- CT scans or MRI for lung cancer or other types of cancer

By taking steps to prevent cancer and getting screened regularly, you can help protect yourself and your loved ones from this devastating disease. It's important to be proactive about your health and to make cancer prevention and early detection a priority. Together, we can work towards a future where cancer is no longer a major threat to our health and well-being.

Chapter 1: Understanding Cancer Types
Explanation of the concept of cancer and how it develops

Cancer is a term used to describe a group of diseases that occur when cells in the body begin to grow uncontrollably. Normally, cells grow and divide in an orderly way, but in cancer, this process goes awry, and cells divide and grow uncontrollably, forming a mass of tissue called a tumor.

Cancer can start in any part of the body and can spread to other parts of the body if not treated. There are many different types of cancer, and each type can develop differently depending on the organ or tissue where it starts.

Cancer can develop due to a combination of genetic and environmental factors. For example, mutations or changes in certain genes can increase the risk of developing cancer. These genetic changes can be inherited from a parent or acquired over a person's lifetime due to exposure to certain carcinogens, such as tobacco smoke, radiation, or certain chemicals.

Additionally, cancer can be caused by lifestyle factors such as a poor diet, lack of exercise, and excessive alcohol consumption. Exposure to viruses and bacteria can also increase the risk of developing certain types of cancer.

It's important to understand how cancer develops so that we can better prevent it and detect it early. Early detection is crucial, as it can lead to more successful treatment outcomes. Knowing the risk factors and symptoms of different types of cancer can help individuals identify potential warning signs and seek medical attention promptly.

By learning more about cancer and how it develops, readers can take steps to reduce their risk of developing cancer and detect it early if it does occur. The following chapters will provide an in-depth look at different types of cancer, their causes, symptoms, and treatment options.

Overview of the different types of cancer, including carcinomas, sarcomas, leukemias, and lymphomas

Cancer is a disease that affects millions of people worldwide. It is caused by the abnormal growth of cells in the body that can form tumors or invade other tissues. There are many different types of cancer, each with its own characteristics and treatment options. In this chapter, we will provide an overview of the most common types of cancer: carcinomas, sarcomas, leukemias, and lymphomas.

Carcinomas are the most common type of cancer and originate in the epithelial cells that make up the body's tissues and organs. There are many different subtypes of carcinomas, such as basal cell carcinoma, squamous cell carcinoma, and adenocarcinoma. Basal cell carcinoma and squamous cell carcinoma are the most common types of skin cancer, while adenocarcinoma can occur in various organs, including the breast, lung, and prostate. Carcinomas can be slow-growing or aggressive, and they can metastasize, or spread, to other parts of the body.

Sarcomas are less common than carcinomas and originate in the body's connective tissues, such as bones, muscles, and cartilage. There are many different subtypes of sarcomas, such as osteosarcoma, chondrosarcoma, and liposarcoma. Osteosarcoma is a bone cancer that commonly affects children and young adults, while liposarcoma is a soft tissue cancer that commonly affects older adults. Sarcomas can be difficult to diagnose and treat, and they can also metastasize to other parts of the body.

Leukemias are cancers that originate in the blood-forming cells in the bone marrow. There are four main types of leukemias: acute lymphoblastic leukemia (ALL), chronic lymphocytic leukemia (CLL), acute myeloid leukemia (AML), and chronic myeloid leukemia (CML). ALL and AML are more common in children, while CLL and CML are more common in adults. Leukemias can be aggressive and rapidly progressing or slow-growing and chronic. Symptoms can include fatigue, fever, and anemia.

Lymphomas are cancers that originate in the lymphatic system, which is part of the immune system. There are two main types of lymphomas: Hodgkin lymphoma and non-Hodgkin lymphoma. Hodgkin lymphoma is characterized by the presence of Reed-Sternberg cells, which are abnormal cells found in the lymph nodes. Non-Hodgkin lymphoma is a diverse group of cancers that can affect any part of the body, including the lymph nodes, bone marrow, and organs. Lymphomas can be slow-growing or aggressive, and they can also spread to other parts of the body.

It's important to note that there are many other types of cancer beyond these four main categories, such as brain cancer, pancreatic cancer, and ovarian cancer. Each type of cancer has its own unique characteristics and treatment options. By understanding the different types of cancer, individuals can better educate themselves and their loved ones on how to prevent and detect cancer early on.

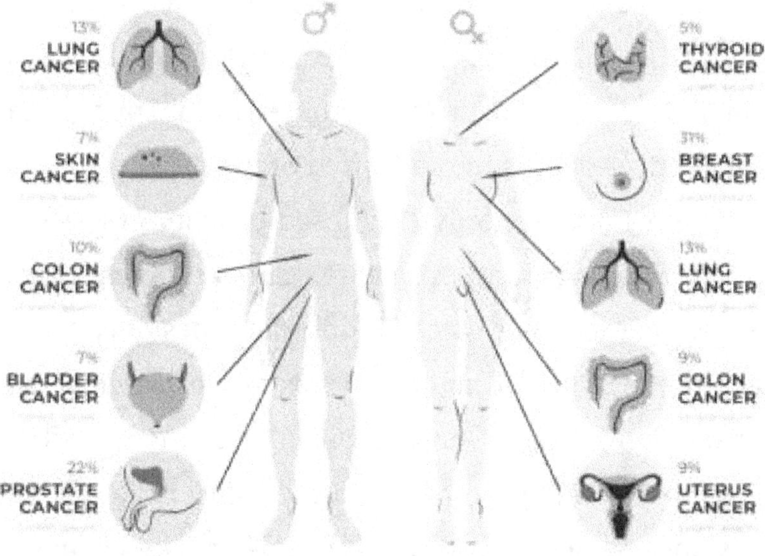

This picture shows the most common types of cancer by gender and their location in the body. It also provides the percentage of possibility for each cancer type. It helps readers understand the prevalence of different types of cancer and how it differs between genders.

Discussion of the prevalence and incidence of different types of cancer

Cancer is a devastating disease that can impact anyone at any time. It is important to understand the prevalence and incidence of different types of cancer so that we can better understand the impact of this disease on our lives and communities.

According to the American Cancer Society, cancer is the second leading cause of death in the United States. In 2022, it is estimated that there will be approximately 1.9 million new cases of cancer diagnosed and approximately 609,640 cancer deaths in the United States.

The most commonly diagnosed cancers in the United States are breast, lung, prostate, and colorectal cancer. However, the incidence rates of different types of cancer vary by age, gender, and ethnicity. For example, women have a higher incidence rate of breast cancer than men, while men have a higher incidence rate of prostate cancer than women.

Cancer incidence rates also vary by geographic location. Some areas have higher rates of certain types of cancer due to environmental factors, such as exposure to pollution or occupational hazards. For example, residents of some parts of the country may be at higher risk of developing lung cancer due to exposure to air pollution or smoking.

It is important to note that while some risk factors for cancer, such as age and genetics, cannot be controlled, there are many lifestyle factors that can be modified to reduce the risk of cancer. These include avoiding tobacco and excessive alcohol consumption, maintaining a healthy diet and weight, staying physically active, and protecting yourself from the sun.

By understanding the prevalence and incidence of different types of cancer, we can better understand the impact of this disease on our lives and communities, and take steps to reduce our risk and prevent the spread of cancer.

Explanation of the role of genetics and other risk factors in the development of cancer

Cancer is a complex disease that can arise from a variety of factors, including genetics, lifestyle, and environmental factors. In this chapter, we will explore the role of genetics and other risk factors in the development of cancer.

Genetics can play a significant role in the development of cancer. Certain gene mutations can increase an individual's risk of developing cancer. For example, mutations in the BRCA1 and BRCA2 genes are associated with an increased risk of breast and ovarian cancer. Other genetic mutations may be inherited or may occur spontaneously and increase the risk of other types of cancer.

In addition to genetics, lifestyle factors such as smoking, diet, and physical activity can also impact an individual's risk of developing cancer. Smoking, for example, is a well-known risk factor for lung cancer, while diets high in red and processed meats are associated with an increased risk of colon cancer.

Exposure to environmental factors such as radiation, chemicals, and pollutants can also increase the risk of cancer. For example, exposure to asbestos is a known risk factor for mesothelioma, while exposure to certain chemicals such as benzene is associated with an increased risk of leukemia.

It is important to note that while certain risk factors may increase an individual's likelihood of developing cancer, it does not necessarily mean that they will develop cancer. Conversely, individuals without any known risk factors may still develop cancer.

Regular screening and early detection are critical in detecting cancer at an early stage when it is most treatable. Individuals with a family history of cancer or other risk factors may benefit from earlier or more frequent screening. In addition, making lifestyle changes such as quitting smoking, adopting a healthier diet, and increasing physical activity can help reduce the risk of cancer.

In conclusion, cancer is a complex disease that can arise from a variety of factors, including genetics, lifestyle, and environmental factors. Understanding these risk factors and taking steps to reduce one's risk through lifestyle changes and regular screening can help prevent or detect cancer at an early stage, improving the chances of successful treatment.

Chapter 2: Carcinomas
In-depth explanation of the different subtypes of carcinomas, such as basal cell carcinoma, squamous cell carcinoma, and adenocarcinoma

Carcinomas are a type of cancer that start in the cells that make up the skin or the lining of organs. There are many different subtypes of carcinomas, each with its own unique characteristics and behaviors. In this chapter, we will provide an in-depth explanation of the different subtypes of carcinomas, including basal cell carcinoma, squamous cell carcinoma, and adenocarcinoma.

Basal cell carcinoma is the most common type of skin cancer, accounting for about 80% of all cases. It usually appears on sun-exposed areas of the body, such as the face, scalp, and neck. Basal cell carcinoma is slow-growing and rarely spreads to other parts of the body. It is easily treated with surgery, radiation therapy, or topical medications.

Squamous cell carcinoma is the second most common type of skin cancer. It also usually appears on sun-exposed areas of the body, but can also develop on other parts of the skin or in the lining of organs. Squamous cell carcinoma can grow quickly and spread to other parts of the body if left untreated. It is usually treated with surgery, radiation therapy, or topical medications.

Adenocarcinoma is a type of carcinoma that starts in the glandular cells of the body. It can occur in many different organs, including the lungs, breast, prostate, and colon. Adenocarcinoma can be slow-growing or fast-growing, depending on the location and stage of the cancer. Treatment options include surgery, radiation therapy, chemotherapy, and targeted therapy.

Other subtypes of carcinomas include small cell carcinoma, large cell carcinoma, and transitional cell carcinoma. Small cell carcinoma is a type of lung cancer that grows quickly and is often associated with smoking. Large cell carcinoma is a less common type of lung cancer that can grow quickly and spread to other parts of the body. Transitional cell carcinoma is a type of bladder cancer that starts in the cells lining the bladder.

It is important to note that each subtype of carcinoma can have different risk factors, symptoms, and treatment options. It is important to discuss any concerns or questions with a healthcare provider.

In summary, carcinomas are a type of cancer that start in the cells that make up the skin or lining of organs. Basal cell carcinoma, squamous cell carcinoma, and adenocarcinoma are some of the most common subtypes of carcinomas, each with its own unique characteristics and behaviors. It is important to be aware of the different subtypes of carcinomas and their respective risks and treatment options.

Discussion of the causes and risk factors associated with each subtype

Carcinomas are a type of cancer that starts in the cells that make up the skin or the lining of organs. There are several subtypes of carcinomas, each with its own unique characteristics, causes, and risk factors. In this chapter, we will take an in-depth look at these subtypes and explore the causes and risk factors associated with each one.

Basal cell carcinoma is the most common subtype of carcinoma, accounting for approximately 80% of all skin cancers. It develops in the basal cells that are located in the deepest layer of the epidermis. The primary cause of basal cell carcinoma is overexposure to the sun or other sources of ultraviolet radiation. Other risk factors include a family history of skin cancer, fair skin, and a weakened immune system.

Squamous cell carcinoma is the second most common subtype of carcinoma, accounting for approximately 16% of all skin cancers. It develops in the squamous cells that are located in the middle layer of the epidermis. Like basal cell carcinoma, overexposure to the sun or other sources of ultraviolet radiation is the primary cause of squamous cell carcinoma. Other risk factors include a history of skin cancer, fair skin, and a weakened immune system.

Adenocarcinoma is a subtype of carcinoma that develops in the glandular cells that line organs such as the lungs, pancreas, and prostate. The causes and risk factors associated with adenocarcinoma vary depending on the organ in which it develops. For example, adenocarcinoma of the lungs is primarily caused by smoking, while adenocarcinoma of the prostate is more common in older men and those with a family history of the disease.

Other subtypes of carcinomas include transitional cell carcinoma, which develops in the cells that line the bladder, and renal cell carcinoma, which develops in the cells of the kidney. The causes and risk factors associated with these subtypes are also unique and will be discussed in detail in later chapters.

It is important to understand the causes and risk factors associated with each subtype of carcinoma because this knowledge can help you take steps to reduce your risk of developing cancer. For example, if you have a family history of skin cancer, you may be more vigilant about protecting your skin from the sun's harmful rays. If you smoke, you may be more likely to develop adenocarcinoma of the lungs, so quitting smoking can significantly reduce your risk.

In summary, carcinomas are a diverse group of cancers with unique causes and risk factors. By understanding these factors, you can take steps to reduce your risk of developing cancer and detect it early if it does occur. It is important to talk to your doctor if you have any concerns about your risk of developing cancer, as they can provide you with personalized advice and recommendations based on your individual health history.

Overview of the symptoms and diagnostic tests used to detect carcinomas

Carcinomas are the most common type of cancer, accounting for approximately 80% of all cases. They develop in epithelial cells, which are the cells that make up the lining of organs and tissues in the body. There are several subtypes of carcinomas, including basal cell carcinoma, squamous cell carcinoma, and adenocarcinoma. While each subtype may have unique symptoms and risk factors, there are some general symptoms and diagnostic tests that can be used to detect carcinomas.

Symptoms of Carcinomas

Symptoms of carcinomas can vary depending on the subtype and the location of the cancer in the body. Some general symptoms that may be present include:

1. Unexplained weight loss: A sudden and unexplained weight loss may be an early sign of some types of carcinomas.

2. Fatigue: A feeling of tiredness that does not go away even after rest may also be an early sign of some types of carcinomas.

3. Skin changes: Changes to the skin, such as a new mole, a sore that doesn't heal, or a change in the color or

texture of the skin, may be a sign of basal or squamous cell carcinoma.

4. Changes in bowel or bladder habits: Changes in bowel or bladder habits, such as constipation or diarrhea, may be a sign of colon or rectal carcinoma.

5. Difficulty swallowing: Difficulty swallowing or pain when swallowing may be a sign of esophageal carcinoma.

6. Persistent cough: A persistent cough that does not go away may be a sign of lung carcinoma.

Diagnostic Tests for Carcinomas

If you are experiencing any of the symptoms mentioned above, or if you are at increased risk for developing a carcinoma, your doctor may recommend diagnostic tests to help detect cancer. Some common tests that may be used include:

1. Biopsy: A biopsy involves the removal of a small sample of tissue from the affected area. The tissue is then examined under a microscope to determine if cancer cells are present.

2. Imaging tests: Imaging tests such as X-rays, CT scans, and MRI scans may be used to create images of the inside of the body. These tests can help doctors identify the location and size of the cancer.

3. Blood tests: Blood tests may be used to check for specific markers that can indicate the presence of cancer.

4. Endoscopy: Endoscopy involves the use of a thin, flexible tube with a camera on the end to examine the inside of the body. This test can be used to examine the esophagus, colon, and other organs.

5. Pap test: A Pap test is a screening test used to detect abnormal cells in the cervix. Abnormal cells may be a sign of cervical cancer.

It is important to note that not all diagnostic tests are necessary for every patient. Your doctor will work with you to determine which tests are most appropriate based on your individual situation. Early detection of carcinomas can lead to more effective treatment and better outcomes, so it is important to be aware of the symptoms and risk factors associated with this type of cancer.

Explanation of the treatments available for each subtype, including surgery, radiation therapy, chemotherapy, and immunotherapy

Carcinomas are the most common type of cancer, and there are several subtypes that require different treatments. Treatment options for carcinomas depend on the subtype and the stage of the cancer.

Surgery is often the first line of treatment for early-stage carcinomas, and it may involve removing the tumor or the affected organ. In some cases, radiation therapy may be used before or after surgery to help shrink the tumor or prevent its recurrence.

Chemotherapy, which uses drugs to kill cancer cells, is another common treatment for carcinomas. It can be given before or after surgery or in combination with radiation therapy. Chemotherapy may be administered orally or intravenously, and the specific drugs used depend on the subtype of carcinoma.

Immunotherapy is a newer treatment option that works by boosting the body's immune system to attack cancer cells. It is often used for advanced or metastatic carcinomas and can have fewer side effects than chemotherapy.

The treatment plan for each subtype of carcinoma is tailored to the individual patient and may involve a combination of these treatments. It's important for patients to work closely with their healthcare team to understand the benefits and risks of each treatment option.

In addition to traditional treatments, there are also complementary and alternative therapies that can be used to help manage symptoms and improve quality of life. These may include acupuncture, massage therapy, and mindfulness meditation.

It's important to note that while treatment can be effective for many cases of carcinoma, it's also important to focus on prevention and early detection. Regular screenings, such as mammograms, Pap tests, and colonoscopies, can help detect carcinomas early when they are more treatable. Quitting smoking, maintaining a healthy weight, and reducing alcohol consumption can also help reduce the risk of developing carcinoma.

Overall, there are many treatment options available for the different subtypes of carcinomas, and the best approach depends on the individual patient's situation. It's important to work closely with a healthcare team to develop a personalized treatment plan and focus on prevention and early detection to improve outcomes.

Chapter 3: Sarcomas
In-depth explanation of the different subtypes of sarcomas, such as osteosarcoma, chondrosarcoma, and liposarcoma

Sarcomas are a type of cancer that originates in the body's connective tissues, such as bone, cartilage, muscle, and fat. There are more than 50 subtypes of sarcomas, which can be classified into two main categories: bone sarcomas and soft tissue sarcomas.

Osteosarcoma is the most common type of bone sarcoma and usually affects teenagers and young adults. It develops in the bone cells and can occur in any bone, but it most commonly affects the long bones of the arms and legs. Symptoms include pain, swelling, and difficulty moving the affected limb. Treatment usually involves chemotherapy and surgery to remove the affected bone and replace it with a prosthesis.

Chondrosarcoma is a rare type of bone cancer that affects the cartilage. It usually develops in adults over the age of 40 and can occur in any bone that contains cartilage, such as the pelvis, ribs, and shoulders. Symptoms include pain and swelling in the affected area. Treatment usually involves surgery to remove the affected bone and surrounding tissue.

Liposarcoma is a type of soft tissue sarcoma that develops in the body's fat cells. It can occur anywhere in the body, but it most commonly affects the limbs, abdomen, and retroperitoneum (the area behind the abdominal cavity). Symptoms include pain, swelling, and a soft lump in the affected area. Treatment usually involves surgery to remove the tumor, followed by radiation therapy and chemotherapy.

Other subtypes of soft tissue sarcomas include leiomyosarcoma (which develops in the smooth muscle), malignant fibrous histiocytoma (which develops in the fibrous tissue), and synovial sarcoma (which develops in the joints).

It is important to note that sarcomas are rare and account for less than 1% of all cancers. However, early detection and treatment are crucial for a good outcome. If you have symptoms such as pain, swelling, or a lump, it is important to see your doctor for an evaluation.

In the next section, we will discuss the causes and risk factors associated with sarcomas.

Discussion of the causes and risk factors associated with each subtype

Sarcomas are a rare type of cancer that affect the connective tissues, such as bone, muscle, and cartilage. There are several subtypes of sarcomas, and each subtype has its own set of causes and risk factors.

One of the most common subtypes of sarcoma is osteosarcoma, which primarily affects the bone. Osteosarcoma is most commonly diagnosed in children and young adults, and the exact causes of this type of cancer are not yet fully understood. However, researchers have identified several risk factors that may increase the likelihood of developing osteosarcoma, including genetic mutations, radiation exposure, and certain bone diseases.

Chondrosarcoma is another subtype of sarcoma that primarily affects the cartilage. This type of cancer is also more commonly diagnosed in adults, particularly those over the age of 40. The exact causes of chondrosarcoma are not yet fully understood, but researchers believe that certain genetic mutations and environmental factors may play a role in its development.

Liposarcoma is a subtype of sarcoma that affects the fat cells in the body. This type of cancer is relatively rare, accounting for less than 1% of all cancer diagnoses.

Researchers are still working to understand the exact causes of liposarcoma, but some known risk factors include certain genetic mutations and exposure to radiation.

Other subtypes of sarcoma include synovial sarcoma, gastrointestinal stromal tumor (GIST), and malignant peripheral nerve sheath tumor (MPNST). Each of these subtypes has its own unique set of causes and risk factors, and researchers are continually working to better understand these factors in order to improve diagnosis and treatment options for patients.

It's important to note that while certain risk factors may increase the likelihood of developing sarcomas, many people who are diagnosed with this type of cancer have no known risk factors at all. Therefore, it's essential to be aware of the common signs and symptoms of sarcomas and to speak with a doctor if you experience any unusual changes in your body. Early detection and treatment can improve outcomes and increase the likelihood of successful treatment.

Overview of the symptoms and diagnostic tests used to detect sarcomas

Sarcomas are a rare type of cancer that can affect the bones, muscles, and other connective tissues in the body. Because of their rarity and the fact that they can present in different ways depending on the location and subtype, it can be difficult to diagnose sarcomas early. In this chapter, we will discuss the symptoms of sarcomas and the diagnostic tests that can be used to detect them.

Symptoms of Sarcomas

The symptoms of sarcomas can vary depending on the location of the cancer and the subtype. Some of the most common symptoms include:

- Pain or swelling in the affected area
- A lump or mass that can be felt under the skin
- Difficulty moving the affected area or joint
- Weakness or numbness in the affected area
- Fatigue or unexplained weight loss
- Fever or night sweats

Because these symptoms can be indicative of many other conditions, it's important to speak with a healthcare provider if you experience any of them for an extended period.

Diagnostic Tests for Sarcomas

If a healthcare provider suspects that a patient may have a sarcoma, they will typically order one or more of the following diagnostic tests:

- Imaging tests: Imaging tests such as X-rays, CT scans, MRI scans, and PET scans can be used to create detailed images of the affected area. These tests can help identify any abnormalities or masses that may be indicative of a sarcoma.

- Biopsy: A biopsy involves taking a small sample of tissue from the affected area and examining it under a microscope. This is the only way to definitively diagnose sarcoma.

- Blood tests: Blood tests can be used to look for certain proteins or markers that are associated with sarcomas. While these tests aren't typically used to diagnose sarcoma, they can be useful in monitoring the progression of the disease.

It's important to note that these tests may not be able to definitively diagnose or rule out sarcoma in every case. In some instances, additional testing may be required to arrive at a diagnosis.

Conclusion

Sarcomas are a rare type of cancer that can be difficult to diagnose early due to their varied symptoms and subtypes.

If you experience any symptoms that may be indicative of sarcoma, it's important to speak with a healthcare provider. Diagnostic tests such as imaging tests and biopsies can be used to help diagnose sarcomas and determine the best course of treatment.

Explanation of the treatments available for each subtype, including surgery, radiation therapy, chemotherapy, and immunotherapy

Sarcomas are a rare type of cancer that can develop in the bones, soft tissues, and organs. Treatment for sarcomas can be complex and depends on the subtype and stage of the cancer.

Surgery is the main treatment option for sarcomas, and the type of surgery performed depends on the size and location of the tumor. For example, if the tumor is in a limb, a surgeon may perform a limb-sparing surgery, which removes the tumor and some surrounding tissue while preserving the function of the limb. In some cases, amputation may be necessary.

Radiation therapy may also be used to treat sarcomas, either alone or in combination with surgery or chemotherapy. Radiation therapy uses high-energy radiation to kill cancer cells and shrink tumors.

Chemotherapy is a type of cancer treatment that uses drugs to kill cancer cells. It can be used before or after surgery, or in combination with radiation therapy. Immunotherapy, a newer treatment option, uses the body's immune system to fight cancer cells.

The choice of treatment for sarcomas depends on several factors, including the subtype and stage of the cancer, the location of the tumor, and the patient's overall health. It is important to discuss treatment options with a healthcare provider and to ask any questions about potential side effects or long-term effects of treatment.

In addition to medical treatments, supportive care is also important for patients with sarcomas. This may include pain management, physical therapy, and emotional support. A multidisciplinary team of healthcare providers, including oncologists, surgeons, radiation therapists, and other specialists, may be involved in a patient's care.

Overall, early detection and prompt treatment can improve the outlook for patients with sarcomas. It is important to maintain regular check-ups with a healthcare provider and to report any unusual symptoms or changes in health to a doctor.

Chapter 4: Leukemias

In-depth explanation of the different types of leukemias, such as acute lymphoblastic leukemia, chronic lymphocytic leukemia, and acute myeloid leukemia

Leukemia is a type of cancer that affects the blood and bone marrow, which are essential components of the body's immune system. In this chapter, we will provide an in-depth explanation of the different types of leukemias, including acute lymphoblastic leukemia (ALL), chronic lymphocytic leukemia (CLL), and acute myeloid leukemia (AML).

Acute lymphoblastic leukemia (ALL) is a type of leukemia that develops in the white blood cells known as lymphocytes. ALL is the most common type of leukemia in children, but it can also affect adults. The cause of ALL is not fully understood, but some risk factors include exposure to radiation, certain genetic disorders, and environmental factors. Symptoms of ALL may include fatigue, fever, infections, and easy bruising or bleeding. The diagnosis of ALL typically involves blood tests, bone marrow biopsy, and imaging tests. Treatment options for ALL include chemotherapy, radiation therapy, and bone marrow transplantation.

Chronic lymphocytic leukemia (CLL) is a type of leukemia that affects the white blood cells known as B-cells. CLL is the most common type of leukemia in adults, and it usually affects people over the age of 50. The cause of CLL is not fully understood, but some risk factors include exposure to certain chemicals, radiation, and genetic factors. Symptoms of CLL may include fatigue, night sweats, swollen lymph nodes, and recurrent infections. The diagnosis of CLL typically involves blood tests and bone marrow biopsy. Treatment options for CLL depend on the stage and severity of the disease, but they may include watchful waiting, chemotherapy, radiation therapy, and targeted therapy.

Acute myeloid leukemia (AML) is a type of leukemia that develops in the white blood cells known as myeloid cells. AML is a rare type of leukemia, but it can be aggressive and progress rapidly if not treated promptly. The cause of AML is not fully understood, but some risk factors include exposure to radiation, certain chemotherapy drugs, and genetic factors. Symptoms of AML may include fatigue, fever, infections, and easy bruising or bleeding. The diagnosis of AML typically involves blood tests, bone marrow biopsy, and imaging tests. Treatment options for AML depend on the stage and severity of the disease, but they may include chemotherapy, radiation therapy, bone marrow transplantation, and targeted therapy.

In summary, leukemia is a type of cancer that affects the blood and bone marrow. In this chapter, we have provided an overview of the different types of leukemias, including acute lymphoblastic leukemia, chronic lymphocytic leukemia, and acute myeloid leukemia. Understanding the causes, symptoms, diagnostic tests, and treatment options for each type of leukemia is critical in managing the disease and improving outcomes for patients. If you or someone you know has been diagnosed with leukemia, it is essential to work closely with your healthcare team to develop a personalized treatment plan that meets your unique needs and circumstances.

Discussion of the causes and risk factors associated with each type

Leukemias are a group of blood cancers that start in the bone marrow, the spongy tissue inside bones where blood cells are made. There are several types of leukemias, each with different causes and risk factors. In this chapter, we will discuss the causes and risk factors associated with each type of leukemia.

Acute Lymphoblastic Leukemia (ALL): ALL is a type of leukemia that affects white blood cells, specifically lymphocytes. It is the most common type of leukemia in children, but it can also occur in adults. The exact cause of ALL is unknown, but it is believed that a combination of genetic and environmental factors may contribute to its development. Risk factors for ALL include exposure to high levels of radiation, certain chemotherapy drugs, and certain genetic disorders.

Chronic Lymphocytic Leukemia (CLL): CLL is a type of leukemia that affects white blood cells, specifically B cells. It is most commonly diagnosed in older adults. The cause of CLL is unknown, but it is believed to be associated with genetic mutations and abnormalities in the immune system. Risk factors for CLL include a family history of the disease, exposure to certain chemicals, and certain viral infections.

Acute Myeloid Leukemia (AML): AML is a type of leukemia that affects white blood cells, specifically myeloid cells. It is more common in older adults, but it can also occur in children. The exact cause of AML is unknown, but it is believed to be associated with genetic mutations and exposure to certain chemicals and radiation. Risk factors for AML include smoking, exposure to benzene and other chemicals, and certain genetic disorders.

Other types of leukemia: There are other types of leukemia that are less common than ALL, CLL, and AML. These include chronic myeloid leukemia (CML), hairy cell leukemia, and adult T-cell leukemia/lymphoma (ATLL). The causes and risk factors for these types of leukemia are not well understood, but they may be associated with genetic mutations and exposure to certain chemicals and viruses.

In conclusion, the causes and risk factors associated with each type of leukemia vary, and not all of them are well understood. However, knowing the risk factors can help individuals make informed decisions about their health and take steps to reduce their risk of developing leukemia. It is important to talk to a healthcare provider if you have concerns about your risk of developing leukemia or if you have any symptoms that could be related to the disease.

Overview of the symptoms and diagnostic tests used to detect leukemias

Leukemia is a type of cancer that affects the blood and bone marrow. It develops when there is an overproduction of abnormal white blood cells, which are responsible for fighting infections in the body. In this section, we will discuss the symptoms and diagnostic tests used to detect different types of leukemias.

Symptoms of Leukemia: The symptoms of leukemia may vary depending on the type of leukemia a person has. The common symptoms of leukemia include:

1. Fatigue: Feeling tired or weak most of the time is a common symptom of leukemia. This happens because the abnormal white blood cells produced by the cancerous cells can't fight off infections effectively.

2. Shortness of breath: When leukemia progresses, it can affect the production of red blood cells, leading to anemia, which can cause shortness of breath.

3. Frequent infections: Leukemia affects the immune system, making it difficult for the body to fight off infections. As a result, people with leukemia may get sick often.

4. Bruising and bleeding: Leukemia can interfere with the production of platelets, which are responsible for blood

clotting. This can lead to bruising, bleeding gums, or nosebleeds.

5. Enlarged lymph nodes: Some types of leukemia can cause the lymph nodes to enlarge, which may cause pain or discomfort.

Diagnostic Tests: If a doctor suspects that a person has leukemia, they will likely perform some diagnostic tests to confirm the diagnosis. The most common tests include:

1. Blood tests: A complete blood count (CBC) is a blood test that measures the number of red blood cells, white blood cells, and platelets in the blood. People with leukemia usually have abnormal blood cell counts.

2. Bone marrow biopsy: This test involves removing a small sample of bone marrow from the hip bone with a needle. The sample is then examined under a microscope to check for cancerous cells.

3. Imaging tests: Imaging tests such as X-rays, CT scans, or MRI scans can help doctors see the size and location of any tumors caused by leukemia.

4. Cytogenetic testing: This test involves analyzing the chromosomes in cancer cells to see if they have any abnormalities.

5. Lumbar puncture: This test involves removing a small amount of cerebrospinal fluid (CSF) from the spine to

check for cancer cells. This test is often done if leukemia has spread to the brain or spinal cord.

In conclusion, early detection of leukemia is essential to increase the chances of successful treatment. If you are experiencing any of the symptoms mentioned above, it is essential to speak to a doctor as soon as possible. Your doctor can perform the necessary tests to determine if you have leukemia and start treatment promptly.

Explanation of the treatments available for each type, including chemotherapy, radiation therapy, bone marrow transplantation, and immunotherapy

Leukemia is a type of cancer that affects the blood and bone marrow, the spongy tissue inside bones where blood cells are produced. There are different types of leukemias, and treatment depends on the type and stage of the disease.

Chemotherapy is a common treatment for leukemia, and it involves the use of drugs to kill cancer cells. The drugs are usually given intravenously or taken orally. Chemotherapy can have side effects such as nausea, vomiting, hair loss, and fatigue, but these side effects can often be managed with medication or lifestyle changes.

Radiation therapy is another treatment option for leukemia, and it involves using high-energy radiation to kill cancer cells. Radiation therapy is often used in combination with chemotherapy. Side effects of radiation therapy can include skin irritation, fatigue, and an increased risk of infection.

Bone marrow transplantation is a procedure where a person receives healthy stem cells to replace their own diseased bone marrow. This can be done using stem cells from a donor or from the patient's own bone marrow. A bone marrow transplant can be a very effective treatment for leukemia, but it is also a complex and risky procedure.

Immunotherapy is a newer type of cancer treatment that works by stimulating the body's immune system to fight cancer cells. Immunotherapy drugs work differently than chemotherapy drugs and can have fewer side effects. They can be used alone or in combination with other treatments such as chemotherapy.

The choice of treatment for leukemia depends on many factors, including the type of leukemia, the stage of the disease, the person's overall health, and their age. Treatment plans are often individualized and may involve a combination of different treatments. It's important to discuss treatment options with a doctor and to ask questions to fully understand the benefits and risks of each option.

Chapter 5: Lymphomas
In-depth explanation of the different types of lymphomas, such as Hodgkin lymphoma and non-Hodgkin lymphoma

Lymphomas are a type of cancer that affect the lymphatic system, which is a part of the immune system. There are two main types of lymphomas: Hodgkin lymphoma and non-Hodgkin lymphoma.

Hodgkin Lymphoma: Hodgkin lymphoma is a type of lymphoma that is characterized by the presence of a specific type of cell called the Reed-Sternberg cell. This type of lymphoma typically starts in a single lymph node or a group of lymph nodes, and then spreads to other lymph nodes and organs. The cause of Hodgkin lymphoma is not known, but it is thought to be related to changes in the DNA of the lymphocytes, which are a type of white blood cell.

The symptoms of Hodgkin lymphoma may include enlarged lymph nodes, fever, night sweats, fatigue, and unexplained weight loss. To diagnose Hodgkin lymphoma, a doctor may perform a physical examination, blood tests, imaging tests, such as a CT scan or PET scan, and a lymph node biopsy.

The treatment for Hodgkin lymphoma typically involves chemotherapy and/or radiation therapy. Depending on the stage of the cancer and other factors, a bone marrow transplant may also be recommended.

Non-Hodgkin Lymphoma: Non-Hodgkin lymphoma is a group of cancers that affect the lymphatic system but do not involve the Reed-Sternberg cell. There are many different subtypes of non-Hodgkin lymphoma, and they can vary in terms of their aggressiveness and treatment options.

The causes of non-Hodgkin lymphoma are not well understood, but they may be related to genetic mutations or exposure to certain environmental factors, such as radiation, chemicals, or viruses.

The symptoms of non-Hodgkin lymphoma can vary depending on the subtype, but may include enlarged lymph nodes, fever, night sweats, fatigue, and unexplained weight loss. To diagnose non-Hodgkin lymphoma, a doctor may perform a physical examination, blood tests, imaging tests, such as a CT scan or PET scan, and a lymph node biopsy.

The treatment for non-Hodgkin lymphoma depends on the subtype and the stage of the cancer. Treatment options may include chemotherapy, radiation therapy, targeted therapy, and immunotherapy. In some cases, a bone marrow transplant may also be recommended.

Overall, the key to successfully treating lymphomas is early detection and diagnosis, so it is important to seek medical attention if you experience any symptoms or have concerns about your risk for these types of cancers.

Discussion of the causes and risk factors associated with each type

Lymphoma is a type of cancer that affects the lymphatic system, which is a part of the immune system. There are two main types of lymphomas: Hodgkin lymphoma and non-Hodgkin lymphoma. The causes of lymphoma are not yet fully understood, but there are some known risk factors that increase the likelihood of developing the disease.

One of the main risk factors for lymphoma is age, as the disease is more common in people over 60 years old. Another risk factor is a weakened immune system, which can be caused by certain medical conditions, such as HIV or autoimmune diseases, or by treatments such as chemotherapy. Exposure to certain chemicals and radiation has also been linked to an increased risk of lymphoma.

In addition to these risk factors, there are some genetic factors that can increase the likelihood of developing lymphoma. For example, some people have inherited genetic mutations that make them more susceptible to the disease.

It's important to remember that having one or more risk factors does not necessarily mean that a person will develop lymphoma. Conversely, some people may develop the disease without any known risk factors.

If you are concerned about your risk of developing lymphoma, talk to your doctor. They can help you understand your individual risk factors and recommend appropriate screening or preventive measures.

Lymphomas are cancers that affect the lymphatic system, which is a crucial part of the body's immune system. This chapter will provide an overview of the different types of lymphomas, their symptoms, and diagnostic tests used to detect them.

Types of Lymphoma: There are two main types of lymphoma - Hodgkin lymphoma and non-Hodgkin lymphoma. Hodgkin lymphoma is named after Dr. Thomas Hodgkin, who first described the disease in 1832. It is characterized by the presence of Reed-Sternberg cells, which are large, abnormal cells found in the lymph nodes. Non-Hodgkin lymphoma, on the other hand, refers to all lymphomas that do not have Reed-Sternberg cells.

Symptoms of Lymphoma: The symptoms of lymphoma can vary depending on the type of lymphoma, the location of the cancer, and the stage of the disease. Some common symptoms of lymphoma include:

- Swollen lymph nodes, which are usually painless
- Fatigue
- Fever
- Night sweats
- Unexplained weight loss

- Itchy skin

- Abdominal pain or swelling

It is important to note that these symptoms can be caused by other conditions as well, so it is essential to consult a healthcare provider for an accurate diagnosis.

Diagnostic Tests: If lymphoma is suspected, the healthcare provider may order one or more diagnostic tests to confirm the diagnosis. Some common tests used to diagnose lymphoma include:

- Biopsy: A sample of tissue is removed from the affected lymph node and examined under a microscope to look for cancer cells.

- Blood tests: Blood tests can help identify abnormalities in the blood cells, which can be indicative of lymphoma.

- Imaging tests: Imaging tests, such as X-rays, CT scans, MRI, or PET scans, can help detect the presence and location of cancerous lymph nodes.

Treatment Options: The treatment for lymphoma depends on the type of lymphoma, its stage, and the individual's overall health. The main treatment options for lymphoma include:

- Chemotherapy: Chemotherapy uses drugs to kill cancer cells and can be given orally or intravenously.

- Radiation therapy: Radiation therapy uses high-energy radiation to kill cancer cells and can be used alone or in combination with chemotherapy.

- Immunotherapy: Immunotherapy helps the immune system to fight cancer by targeting specific proteins on cancer cells.

- Stem cell transplantation: Stem cell transplantation involves replacing the patient's bone marrow with healthy stem cells, which can help produce healthy blood cells.

Conclusion: In summary, lymphoma is a type of cancer that affects the lymphatic system. It can cause a range of symptoms, and the diagnosis is confirmed through diagnostic tests such as biopsy, blood tests, and imaging tests. The treatment options depend on the type of lymphoma and the stage of the disease, but they may include chemotherapy, radiation therapy, immunotherapy, or stem cell transplantation. Early diagnosis and treatment can improve the prognosis for individuals with lymphoma, and it is essential to consult a healthcare provider if you experience any symptoms.

Explanation of the treatments available for each type, including chemotherapy, radiation therapy, targeted therapy, and immunotherapy

Lymphomas are cancers that start in the cells of the immune system called lymphocytes. There are two main types of lymphoma: Hodgkin lymphoma (HL) and non-Hodgkin lymphoma (NHL). Treatment options for lymphomas depend on the type and stage of the cancer, as well as the individual patient's health status and preferences.

Chemotherapy: Chemotherapy is the use of drugs to kill cancer cells. Chemotherapy is often used as the first-line treatment for many types of NHL. It may also be used as a part of the treatment for HL. Chemotherapy drugs can be given orally, intravenously, or injected directly into the cerebrospinal fluid. Chemotherapy can cause side effects, such as nausea, vomiting, hair loss, and increased risk of infections.

Radiation therapy: Radiation therapy uses high-energy radiation to kill cancer cells. It may be used alone or in combination with chemotherapy for the treatment of HL and some types of NHL. Radiation therapy is typically delivered externally using a machine that aims the radiation beams at the affected area of the body. Side effects of radiation therapy include skin irritation, fatigue, and increased risk of infections.

Targeted therapy: Targeted therapy drugs work by targeting specific molecules in cancer cells that are necessary for their growth and survival. They can be used to treat certain types of NHL, including follicular lymphoma, mantle cell lymphoma, and diffuse large B-cell lymphoma. Targeted therapy drugs are usually given intravenously and can cause side effects such as skin rash, diarrhea, and high blood pressure.

Immunotherapy: Immunotherapy drugs are designed to help the body's immune system to recognize and attack cancer cells. They may be used alone or in combination with chemotherapy or targeted therapy for the treatment of some types of NHL, including follicular lymphoma, mantle cell lymphoma, and diffuse large B-cell lymphoma. Immunotherapy drugs can cause side effects such as fever, chills, and fatigue.

Stem cell transplantation: Stem cell transplantation is a procedure in which healthy stem cells are collected from the patient or a donor and transplanted into the patient's body after high-dose chemotherapy or radiation therapy. Stem cell transplantation is often used as a treatment option for NHL that has not responded to other treatments. This procedure can cause serious side effects, such as infections and graft-versus-host disease.

In conclusion, there are several treatment options available for lymphomas, including chemotherapy, radiation therapy, targeted therapy, immunotherapy, and stem cell transplantation. Each treatment has its own benefits and risks, and the choice of treatment will depend on several factors, including the type and stage of the cancer, the patient's health status, and personal preferences. It is important to discuss the available treatment options with a healthcare provider to make an informed decision about the best course of action for each individual case.

Chapter 6: Current Research and Treatment Options

Discussion of the latest research and advances in cancer treatment

Cancer research is constantly evolving, and new treatments are being developed all the time. In recent years, there have been significant advances in cancer treatment, with many new drugs and therapies becoming available. This chapter will provide an overview of the latest research and advances in cancer treatment.

Immunotherapy One of the most exciting areas of cancer research is immunotherapy. This approach harnesses the power of the immune system to fight cancer. Researchers are developing a range of immunotherapies, including checkpoint inhibitors, CAR-T cell therapy, and cancer vaccines. These treatments work by either stimulating the immune system or enhancing its ability to recognize and attack cancer cells.

Precision Medicine Another promising area of research is precision medicine, which uses a patient's individual genetic profile to determine the most effective treatment for their cancer. By analyzing the genetic mutations present in a patient's cancer cells, doctors can identify targeted therapies that are tailored to the specific genetic abnormalities of the tumor. This approach can result in more effective treatment and fewer side effects.

Liquid Biopsies Traditionally, cancer is diagnosed through a tissue biopsy, which involves removing a sample of the tumor and analyzing it in the laboratory. However, researchers are now exploring the use of liquid biopsies, which involve analyzing a patient's blood or other bodily fluids for cancer cells and genetic abnormalities. This approach has the potential to provide earlier and less invasive diagnosis, as well as monitoring of cancer progression and treatment response.

Nanotechnology Another area of research that holds promise for cancer treatment is nanotechnology. Nanoparticles can be designed to deliver drugs directly to cancer cells, while avoiding healthy cells. This approach can increase the effectiveness of chemotherapy and reduce side effects. Researchers are also exploring the use of nanotechnology for imaging and diagnosis.

Clinical Trials Clinical trials are an essential part of cancer research, as they are designed to test new drugs and treatments in humans. Participation in a clinical trial may give patients access to treatments that are not yet available to the general public. Patients who are interested in participating in a clinical trial should discuss the option with their doctor.

Conclusion While cancer remains a significant health challenge, advances in research and treatment are offering new hope for patients. Immunotherapy, precision medicine, liquid biopsies, nanotechnology, and clinical trials are just a few of the areas where progress is being made. As research continues, it is hoped that even more effective treatments will become available, leading to improved outcomes for cancer patients.

Overview of new and emerging therapies, such as CAR T-cell therapy and targeted therapy

As research into cancer treatment advances, new and emerging therapies are being developed that show promise in improving outcomes for patients. Two of these therapies are CAR T-cell therapy and targeted therapy.

CAR T-cell therapy is a form of immunotherapy that uses the patient's own immune cells, called T cells, to attack cancer cells. In this therapy, T cells are taken from the patient's blood and modified in a laboratory to produce chimeric antigen receptors (CARs) on their surface. These receptors enable the T cells to recognize and bind to specific proteins on cancer cells, which then triggers the T cells to attack and destroy the cancer cells. CAR T-cell therapy has been approved for the treatment of certain types of blood cancers, such as acute lymphoblastic leukemia and some types of lymphoma.

Targeted therapy, on the other hand, is a type of cancer treatment that uses drugs to target specific molecules or proteins that are involved in the growth and spread of cancer cells. Unlike chemotherapy, which can kill both cancerous and healthy cells, targeted therapy specifically targets cancer cells and spares healthy cells. There are different types of targeted therapy, such as monoclonal antibodies, small molecule inhibitors, and immune checkpoint inhibitors. Monoclonal antibodies are laboratory-produced molecules that can mimic the immune system's ability to fight cancer by binding to specific proteins on the surface of cancer cells and triggering an immune response. Small molecule inhibitors, on the other hand, work by blocking the activity of specific molecules or proteins that are involved in the growth and spread of cancer cells. Immune checkpoint inhibitors work by blocking proteins that prevent the immune system from attacking cancer cells.

Both CAR T-cell therapy and targeted therapy offer new and promising options for cancer treatment. However, they are still relatively new and their long-term effectiveness and potential side effects are still being studied. As with any cancer treatment, it is important to discuss the risks and benefits of these therapies with your doctor to determine if they are appropriate for your specific situation.

In addition to CAR T-cell therapy and targeted therapy, there are also other emerging therapies that are currently being studied in clinical trials. These include:

- Cancer vaccines: Vaccines that stimulate the immune system to recognize and attack cancer cells.

- Oncolytic viruses: Viruses that are modified to specifically infect and kill cancer cells.

- Gene therapy: Therapy that involves introducing new genes into a patient's cells to treat or prevent disease.

- Nanoparticle-based therapies: Therapies that use tiny particles to deliver drugs directly to cancer cells.

These therapies are still in the early stages of development, but they hold promise for the future of cancer treatment. As research into these therapies continues, it is hoped that they will provide more effective and less toxic treatment options for cancer patients.

Explanation of the importance of clinical trials in developing new cancer treatments

Clinical trials are an essential part of developing new cancer treatments. These trials involve testing new drugs, therapies, and medical procedures on human volunteers to determine their safety and effectiveness. The goal of these trials is to identify treatments that are more effective than current ones and to bring new treatments to market that can improve outcomes for cancer patients.

One reason clinical trials are crucial is that cancer is a complex disease, and not all treatments work for everyone. Clinical trials allow researchers to test new treatments on a large and diverse group of people to see if they are effective across different types of cancer and patient populations.

Another reason clinical trials are vital is that they help researchers better understand the biology of cancer. By studying the effects of new treatments on cancer cells and tumors, researchers can gain insights into how cancer develops and progresses. This knowledge can help lead to the development of more effective treatments and ultimately, a cure for cancer.

Participating in a clinical trial can also benefit cancer patients. While there is no guarantee that a new treatment will work, patients who participate in clinical trials often receive close monitoring from medical professionals and may have access to treatments that are not yet available to the general public. Additionally, patients who participate in clinical trials help advance medical research and contribute to the development of new treatments that can benefit future generations.

It is important to note that clinical trials are highly regulated and closely monitored to ensure that the safety and rights of participants are protected. Before a clinical trial can begin, it must receive approval from the appropriate regulatory bodies, such as the FDA. Additionally, participants in clinical trials are closely monitored for potential side effects and complications, and researchers must follow strict protocols to ensure the safety and well-being of participants.

In summary, clinical trials play a critical role in developing new cancer treatments. They help researchers better understand the biology of cancer, identify treatments that are more effective than current ones, and bring new treatments to market that can improve outcomes for cancer patients. While participating in a clinical trial is a personal decision, it can benefit not only the patient but also future generations of cancer patients.

Personal stories and interviews with cancer patients and survivors who have undergone these new treatments

Personal stories and interviews with cancer patients and survivors who have undergone new treatments can provide invaluable insights into the experience of living with cancer and the impact that new treatments can have on patients' lives. By sharing their stories, these individuals can help others who are going through similar experiences and provide hope and encouragement to those who are facing a cancer diagnosis.

One of the most significant benefits of sharing personal stories and interviews with cancer patients and survivors is that it can help reduce the stigma and fear that is often associated with cancer. When people hear about the experiences of others who have faced cancer and come out on the other side, it can help normalize the experience and make it feel less isolating. Hearing about the struggles, triumphs, and emotions that others have experienced can provide a sense of community and support to those who are going through a similar journey.

Additionally, personal stories and interviews with cancer patients and survivors who have undergone new treatments can help raise awareness about the latest research and treatment options available. By sharing their experiences with new therapies such as CAR T-cell therapy and targeted therapy, patients can help others understand the potential benefits of these treatments and encourage them to talk to their doctors about whether they may be appropriate.

Moreover, hearing personal stories and interviews with cancer patients and survivors can help healthcare providers better understand the needs of their patients. By gaining insights into the experiences of cancer patients, doctors, nurses, and other healthcare providers can develop more compassionate and patient-centered care plans that take into account the emotional and psychological needs of cancer patients and their families.

Overall, personal stories and interviews with cancer patients and survivors who have undergone new treatments can provide a wealth of knowledge and inspiration to those who are facing cancer or caring for a loved one with cancer. These stories can help reduce stigma and fear, raise awareness about new treatment options, and help healthcare providers better understand the needs of their patients. By sharing their experiences, cancer patients and survivors can help others navigate the difficult journey of living with cancer and provide hope and encouragement for a better future.

Conclusion
Recap of key points covered in the book

In conclusion, this book has aimed to provide readers with a comprehensive understanding of different types of cancer, including their symptoms, treatments, and personal experiences from survivors and families. Throughout the book, we have discussed the emotional impact of a cancer diagnosis, the role of genetics and other risk factors in cancer development, and in-depth explanations of the different subtypes of cancer.

Chapter 1 provided a foundational understanding of cancer and the various types of cancer, including carcinomas, sarcomas, leukemias, and lymphomas. In Chapters 2-5, we delved into each subtype, discussing their causes, symptoms, diagnostic tests, and treatments available.

We have also highlighted the importance of cancer prevention and early detection efforts, as well as the latest research and advances in cancer treatment. In Chapter 6, we discussed the latest therapies and emerging treatments, such as CAR T-cell therapy and targeted therapy. We also explained the importance of clinical trials in developing new cancer treatments and shared personal stories and interviews with cancer patients and survivors who have undergone these new treatments.

It is important to remember that cancer is a complex disease that affects millions of people around the world. There is no one-size-fits-all approach to treating cancer, and each individual's journey will be unique. However, through this book, we hope to provide readers with the knowledge and understanding to navigate the difficult journey of cancer with a sense of empowerment and hope.

In summary, this book has covered the following key points:

Understanding different types of cancer, including their symptoms, causes, and treatments

The emotional impact of a cancer diagnosis and the importance of support

The role of genetics and other risk factors in cancer development

The latest research and advances in cancer treatment, including emerging therapies and clinical trials

Personal stories and interviews with cancer patients and survivors who have undergone these new treatments.

We hope that this book has been a valuable resource for readers seeking to understand and demystify cancer. Remember, early detection and prevention efforts are crucial, and there is always hope for the future of cancer research and treatment. We encourage readers to take action and become advocates for their own health and the health of their loved ones. Together, we can continue to make progress in the fight against cancer.

Call to action for continued cancer prevention and early detection efforts

The fight against cancer is ongoing, and it requires the effort and commitment of everyone to make a significant impact. We have learned throughout this book about the various types of cancer, their risk factors, symptoms, and available treatments. However, we cannot overlook the importance of prevention and early detection efforts.

Prevention is key to reducing the incidence of cancer. There are several lifestyle changes that can be made to reduce the risk of cancer, including maintaining a healthy weight, eating a balanced diet, exercising regularly, limiting alcohol intake, and avoiding tobacco products. It is crucial to note that some cancers, such as those caused by genetic mutations, cannot be prevented through lifestyle changes. Still, early detection can increase the chances of successful treatment and cure.

Early detection is crucial in the fight against cancer. Routine screenings for cancers such as breast, colon, cervical, and lung can detect cancer in its early stages, increasing the chances of successful treatment. It is essential to discuss with your doctor the appropriate screening recommendations for your age and family history.

In addition to personal efforts to reduce the risk of cancer, community-based efforts are crucial in promoting cancer prevention and early detection. Community outreach programs, educational initiatives, and cancer awareness campaigns can all play a significant role in reducing cancer incidence and mortality rates.

We all have a part to play in the fight against cancer. It is crucial to take charge of our health, adopt healthy habits, and stay informed about cancer prevention and early detection efforts. By working together and committing to these efforts, we can make significant strides in reducing the impact of cancer on individuals, families, and communities.

Let us continue to raise awareness about cancer prevention and early detection, advocate for increased funding for cancer research, and support those affected by cancer in their journey towards recovery. Together, we can make a difference.

Hope for the future of cancer research and treatment

As we come to the end of this book, it's important to remember that there is always hope for the future of cancer research and treatment. The field of oncology is constantly evolving, and new breakthroughs are being made every day. In this section, we will discuss some of the reasons why we can remain hopeful about the future of cancer care.

First and foremost, it's important to recognize that the medical community has made tremendous progress in the fight against cancer. We now have a much deeper understanding of the disease than ever before, and we have more tools and technologies at our disposal to detect and treat it. Thanks to advances in genetic research, we are now able to develop targeted therapies that can specifically attack cancer cells, while leaving healthy cells unharmed. These targeted therapies have already been shown to be incredibly effective in some cases, and we can expect even more progress in this area in the years to come.

Another reason to be hopeful is the ongoing research into immunotherapy. This innovative approach to cancer treatment harnesses the power of the body's own immune system to fight cancer. With immunotherapy, doctors are able to boost the body's natural ability to recognize and attack cancer cells, leading to impressive results in some patients. Although there is still much to learn about how best to use immunotherapy in the fight against cancer, the potential is clearly there for this to be a game-changer.

We should also be optimistic about the role that technology will play in the future of cancer care. Advances in imaging technology, for example, have already made it possible to detect cancers earlier than ever before. And as our understanding of the disease grows, we can expect to see even more innovative technologies that will help us to better diagnose and treat cancer. For example, some researchers are exploring the use of artificial intelligence to help identify patterns in cancer data that might be missed by human doctors.

Finally, we should remember that cancer survivors are living proof that progress is being made every day. Thanks to advancements in cancer treatment, more people than ever are surviving the disease and living long, healthy lives. While there is still much work to be done, we should take heart in the knowledge that we are making progress, and that the future is bright.

In conclusion, we should remain hopeful about the future of cancer research and treatment. With ongoing advances in genetics, immunotherapy, technology, and more, we can expect to see continued progress in the fight against cancer. And as we move forward, we should be inspired by the many cancer survivors who are living proof that progress is being made every day. Together, we can work towards a future in which cancer is no longer a life-threatening disease, but a manageable condition that can be successfully treated and cured.

Explanation of the resources available for cancer patients and their families

In this final section, we will provide an overview of the resources available for cancer patients and their families. A cancer diagnosis can be overwhelming, but there are many resources available to help patients and their loved ones cope with the emotional and practical challenges of cancer.

Support groups: Many cancer patients find comfort and understanding by joining support groups. These groups can provide emotional support, practical advice, and a sense of community.

Counseling services: Professional counseling can help patients and their families cope with the emotional challenges of cancer. Counseling services may be available through hospitals, cancer centers, or community organizations.

Financial assistance: Cancer treatment can be expensive, and many patients face financial challenges during their treatment. There are a number of organizations that provide financial assistance to cancer patients and their families, including the American Cancer Society and CancerCare.

Transportation assistance: Cancer treatment often requires frequent visits to the hospital or treatment center, which can be difficult for patients who do not have transportation. Some organizations provide transportation assistance to help patients get to and from their appointments.

Home care services: Patients who require assistance with daily activities may benefit from home care services. These services can provide help with tasks such as bathing, dressing, and meal preparation.

Clinical trials: Clinical trials are research studies that test new cancer treatments. Patients who participate in clinical trials may have access to cutting-edge treatments that are not yet available to the general public.

In addition to these resources, patients and their families may benefit from online resources, such as cancer support groups and educational materials. The American Cancer Society, CancerCare, and the National Cancer Institute all offer a wealth of information and resources online.

In conclusion, cancer is a complex and challenging disease, but patients and their families do not have to face it alone. There are many resources available to provide emotional support, financial assistance, and practical help to those affected by cancer. By taking advantage of these resources and working together, we can continue to make progress in the fight against cancer.

THE END

Key Terms and Definitions

To help you better understand the language and concepts related to aging and older adults, below you will find a list of key terms and their definitions.

Cancer: A group of diseases characterized by the uncontrolled growth and spread of abnormal cells in the body.

Carcinoma: A type of cancer that begins in the cells that make up the skin or the lining of organs, such as the lungs, liver, or kidneys.

Sarcoma: A type of cancer that begins in the connective tissue of the body, such as bone, muscle, or cartilage.

Leukemia: A type of cancer that affects the blood and bone marrow, and is characterized by the production of abnormal white blood cells.

Lymphoma: A type of cancer that affects the lymphatic system, which is responsible for fighting infections and diseases.

Symptoms: The physical or mental manifestations of a disease or condition that are experienced by the patient.

Diagnosis: The process of determining the presence and nature of a disease or condition, often through medical tests and evaluations.

Treatment: The medical interventions and therapies used to manage, cure, or alleviate the symptoms of a disease or condition.

Surgery: A medical procedure in which a surgeon removes or repairs a part of the body that is affected by disease or injury.

Radiation therapy: A type of cancer treatment that uses high-energy radiation to kill cancer cells or shrink tumors.

Chemotherapy: A type of cancer treatment that uses drugs to kill cancer cells or prevent them from dividing and growing.

Immunotherapy: A type of cancer treatment that uses the body's immune system to fight cancer cells.

Clinical trials: Medical research studies that test the safety and effectiveness of new treatments, drugs, or procedures on human subjects.

Prevention: Actions taken to reduce the risk of developing a disease or condition.

Early detection: The identification of a disease or condition in its early stages, often through screening or testing, which can increase the chances of successful treatment and recovery.

Supporting Materials

Introduction:

"Cancer Facts & Figures 2022." American Cancer Society.

https://www.cancer.org/content/dam/cancer-
org/research/cancer-facts-and-statistics/annual-cancer-
facts-and-figures/2022/cancer-facts-and-figures-2022.pdf

Chapter 1:

"What Is Cancer?" National Cancer Institute.

https://www.cancer.gov/about-cancer/understanding/what-
is-cancer

"Understanding Cancer." Cancer.Net.

https://www.cancer.net/cancer-types

Chapter 2:

"Carcinoma." MedlinePlus.

https://medlineplus.gov/ency/article/001279.htm

"Skin Cancer Types." American Cancer Society.

https://www.cancer.org/cancer/skin-cancer/about/skin-
cancer-types.html

Chapter 3:

"Sarcoma." Mayo Clinic.

https://www.mayoclinic.org/diseases-
conditions/sarcoma/symptoms-causes/syc-20351072

"Bone Cancer Types." American Cancer Society. https://www.cancer.org/cancer/bone-cancer/about/bone-cancer-types.html

Chapter 4:

"Leukemia." Mayo Clinic. https://www.mayoclinic.org/diseases-conditions/leukemia/symptoms-causes/syc-20374373

"Types of Childhood Cancer." St. Jude Children's Research Hospital. https://www.stjude.org/disease/leukemia-all/understanding-leukemia/types-of-leukemia.html

Chapter 5:

"Lymphoma." Mayo Clinic. https://www.mayoclinic.org/diseases-conditions/lymphoma/symptoms-causes/syc-20352638

"Hodgkin Lymphoma." American Cancer Society. https://www.cancer.org/cancer/hodgkin-lymphoma/about/hodgkin-lymphoma.html

Chapter 6:

"Cancer Treatment." National Cancer Institute. https://www.cancer.gov/about-cancer/treatment

"New Cancer Treatments." American Cancer Society. https://www.cancer.org/treatment/treatments-and-side-effects/new-cancer-treatments.html

Conclusion:

"Preventing Cancer." Centers for Disease Control and Prevention. https://www.cdc.gov/cancer/dcpc/prevention/

"Cancer Survivorship." National Cancer Institute. https://www.cancer.gov/about-cancer/coping/survivorship

"Support Programs and Services." CancerCare. https://www.cancercare.org/support_programs

www.ingramcontent.com/pod-product-compliance
Lightning Source LLC
LaVergne TN
LVHW011041200726
843509LV00011B/1326